by Joaquin Mardonez

illustrated by Rosemary Jarman

SCHOOL PUBLISHERS

Printed in China

ISBN 10: 0-15-351536-8
ISBN 13: 978-0-15-351536-1

Ordering Options
ISBN 10: 0-15-351214-8 (Grade 4 Advanced Collection)
ISBN 13: 978-0-15-351214-8 (Grade 4 Advanced Collection)
ISBN 10: 0-15-358126-3 (package of 5)
ISBN 13: 978-0-15-358126-7 (package of 5)

5 6 7 8 9 10 985 12 11 10 09

Jen had never been to a ranch before. When Aunt May and Uncle Josh invited her to spend the summer at their ranch, she couldn't believe her good fortune.

"Wow, Uncle Josh, this certainly is different from the city!" she said.

As they pulled up to *Buena Casa*, which was the name of the ranch, Jen could barely contain her excitement. "When can I ride a horse? Where are all the cattle, and are there other animals here, too?"

"Whoa, slow down. Aunt May is waiting for us, so let's at least say hello to her first!" chuckled Uncle Josh.

"What does *Buena Casa* mean?" asked Jen.

"Good home," replied Uncle Josh.

"I like that," said Jen. "It feels like a good home already."

Aunt May and Uncle Josh took Jen for a tour.
The ranch was a huge, working cattle ranch. It
consisted of many animals and cowhands who kept
the ranch going. Each day, the workers tended the
cattle herd, checked for stray cows, tended to sick
cows, and made sure the fences were in good repair.

As the three drove up to the horse stable, a young
woman appeared on a magnificent horse. "Is this the
new cowgirl?" she smiled kindly at Jen.

"Elena, may I present my niece, Jen," said Aunt
May. "Elena is in charge of the horse stable."

"Oh, when can I ride a horse?" exclaimed Jen.

Elena chuckled and then responded, "Well, you'll
need to learn some basics before we take you out on
the trail."

That afternoon, Elena showed Jen the horses and the tack room where the saddles and bridles were kept. Jen had never seen a horse up close before. "They are so big and a little bit scary, but I would definitely love to learn to ride," she thought.

Just then, a horse galloped up to the stable. Riding the horse was Elena's son, Miguel.

"Miguel, this is Jen," said Elena. "She is from the city, visiting her aunt and uncle for the summer. I hope you will spend some time with her and make her feel at home."

Jen smiled because she was really glad to have a new friend, and perhaps Miguel would even teach her to ride. Then Elena went off to do some chores.

Miguel walked his horse into the stable with Jen following close behind. He unbuckled the saddle and removed it, and then he took a soft brush and began to groom his horse.

"I want to be sure my horse looks perfect for the state fair in August. They have a horse show there, and they even have a junior show for young riders," said Miguel. Then he asked Jen, "Ever ridden a horse before?"

"No, but I really want to learn," she replied.

"Well, you're kind of little, so I don't know whether you could handle one of these big horses," said Miguel.

Jen, being prideful, did not want Miguel to realize that she was nervous about riding. "Oh, I'm not afraid, and I learn extremely quickly," she replied confidently.

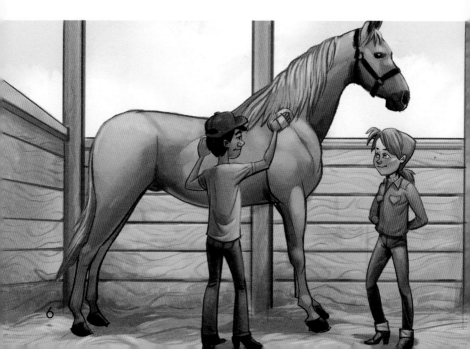

The next day, Jen watched Miguel and some of the kids practice roping. They would get on their horses and swing a lasso in the air. Once the lasso landed over the pole, they would pull the rope closed. Then they would jump off the horse and start all over again. They were practicing for the roping contest at the state fair.

"Ever watch a cowboy throw a lasso before?" Miguel asked, showing off a bit. "The trick is how fast you can do it. All good cowhands know how to lasso and rope."

"I really wish I could learn to ride a horse like that," Jen thought longingly.

Later that day, Elena noticed Jen sitting alone under a tree, looking a bit forlorn. "What's wrong, Jen?" she asked sympathetically.

"Miguel seems to think that I'm too little to ride a horse," Jen replied quietly.

"Come with me. I believe I have something that might make you feel better," said Elena.

She led Jen around to the back stall of the stable, and there stood a larger horse with a smaller horse. The larger horse was a lovely chestnut color, and the smaller horse was the most beautiful and fabulous animal Jen had ever seen.

Elena stroked the smaller horse's nose and told Jen, "This is Moon, and Star here is her daughter. Would you like to pet Star?" she asked.

Slowly, Jen held out her hand and touched the small horse's mane. She had never touched a horse before, and it was such an amazing feeling, she could hardly breathe.

"This horse is very gentle and just the right size for a little girl. Know anyone who might be interested?" Elena asked, her eyes twinkling.

"Oh, Elena, could I?" gushed Jen.

"We'll start first thing in the morning, but first you might want to get acquainted with Star," answered Elena. "One of the most essential things to know is how to take care of your horse, so I'll show you how to brush her."

Elena took a soft brush and began to carefully groom the horse. "It doesn't hurt to slip her a little sugar cube, either," she said.

Shyly, Jen stepped forward, took the brush, and slowly and carefully, she stroked the horse's body. Then she slipped the horse the sugar cube that Elena had placed in her hand.

The very next day, Elena had Star saddled up and ready to go. Elena helped Jen place her foot in the stirrup, and then she was in the saddle! Elena took the horse's bridle and led her slowly around a small corral.

Miguel and his friends watched from behind the fence as Jen beamed with pride.

Day after day, Jen practiced. Sometimes Elena held the bridle, and sometimes Miguel did. They practiced walking and then trotting. After a time, Elena tied a longer rope to the horse's bridle and held it from afar. She let Star circle around her in a canter, which is a smooth easy pace. Then, finally, Star moved into a slow gallop. Jen was a good student and learned incredibly quickly.

"She will be good with horses," thought Elena proudly.

Secretly, Jen intended to enter the junior horse show at the state fair in August, but she could not tell anyone her plan yet, and, of course, she had to learn to ride alone first. She realized that Miguel and his friends would be entering several of the contests. How surprised they would be when they saw her riding Star in the show!

Summer passed quickly, and every day, Jen practiced riding Star. Gradually, she began to ride the little horse on her own, with Elena watching closely behind her. Then one day, when she felt ready, Jen told Elena about her plan. Elena agreed that Jen would be ready for the show.

The state fair was a two-week event at the end of August. Ranchers would enter select cattle, hogs, sheep, and horses in contests.

The junior horse show was to take place the first
day of the fair. That day, while Aunt May, Uncle Josh,
Elena, and Miguel were preparing to go to the fair,
Elena handed Jen a wrapped box.

Jen giggled with delight when she opened the box.
"Oh, this is the most beautiful cowgirl hat I've ever
seen," she said. She snatched the hat from the box and
plopped it on her head so fast that Elena laughed.

The horse show took place in a small corral at one
end of the fairgrounds. Elena saddled up Star, put on her
new hat, and swung up into the saddle. Miguel and his
friends were there. Elena had told them they might want
to come watch the show, but they were surprised to see
Jen as she gave them a little wave.

Jen patted Star, waited for her turn, and then she heard her name being called! She clucked at Star, and off they went. Carefully, she guided Star through a series of movements. Horses and riders were judged on how well they handled each move. They were required to walk, trot, and then canter.

Aunt May and Uncle Josh watched proudly, and Uncle Josh said, "Not bad for a city kid."

Aunt May gave him a poke. "Just remember where I came from," teased Aunt May, recalling her own childhood growing up in the city.

Jen beamed with pride, and at the end of the performance, she tipped her hat to her family and new friends, as Elena, Miguel, and his friends cheered wildly.

Back at the fairground stables, Jen carefully brushed Star. Then Elena and Miguel called to her because it was time to announce the winners.

Jen joined her family in the stands. One by one, the winners were announced, but Jen's name was not one of them. "It's okay, you are a winner to all of us, and having you come to the ranch this summer has been the best thing that has happened in a long time," said Miguel.

Jen couldn't agree more as she thought, "Next summer, I'll definitely win a prize." Then she looked at her aunt and uncle and her new friends. "Well, what are we all waiting for? Let's go to the fair!" Jen shouted, and off they all went.

Think Critically

1. Why does Jen feel left out when she first arrives at the ranch?

2. How did Jen feel when she found out that she did not win a prize?

3. Why is the setting so important to the story?

4. Why do you think Jen keeps it a secret that she wants to enter the junior horse show?

5. Would you like to spend a summer visiting a ranch? Why or why not?

Social Studies

Draw a Poster Find out where and when the state fair takes place in your state and what some of the events are. Make a poster that advertises your state fair. Include the information you found on your poster.

School-Home Connection Ask family members what they would do for a summer vacation if they could do anything. Have each share where he or she would go and why.

Word Count: 1,561